Sample Your Words, See How They Taste

Sample Your Words, See How They Taste

A Lesson In Thinking Before You Speak

Text by
Valeria V. Cordy Cray

Illustrations by
Sabbath Canady and Sojourner Canady

Grandma Grace, when I ask
you a question why do
you take so long to answer?

Well, I do my words like
     I do my cooking.

I gather up my words.
     I mix them together.

Then I sample them
     to see how they "taste."

BAKE 400°
LOVE

8

or do they
burn my face?"

"Will they linger sweet
like chocolate cake. . .

or grip and hurt like
an old toothache?"

"Are they refreshing like a lemonade shower. . .

or strong and bitter like old cauliflower?"

Words can bruise,
words can burn.

Words can heal
and show concern.

"Wow! Should I sample my words?"

Yes, especially when you talk to your brother.

Yesterday I heard you say, "Bentley, you are such a knucklehead! Would you just go away!"

Those words sound really bad!

I see why they made Bentley
feel so sad.

I am sorry that I said
   those things.

But, Grandma Grace,
   I think that "Sample
   Your Words" is a
   grown-up thing.

Excuse me...
You're welcome...
May I
Yes, please...

It might be good
for Moms and Dads.

But it sounds too hard
for me.

I don't think a "sample
your words" person
is one that I can be.

Natalie, my dear,
    this is for everyone.

Pay attention to the words
    you select. Try to choose
    words that show respect.

Meanie
Snob
Friend

You are saying, "Pause!
    Then taste your words.
    Then speak."

That is just too much
    to think about.

I know that when I am tired or
    angry my words just come
    pouring out.

Let's try this. Take a deep breath
    before you speak and ask,
    "Do these words say what

I want to express?"

Then say the words only
    if the answer is YES.

AM TIRED

IGNORANT
JERK
FOOL
IDIOT
ANNOYIN
DORK

Grandma Grace,
    all of this is just too hard.

If I blurt out words that hurt
    can't I just say "I'm sorry?"

Won't that still work?

That is not how words work.
    Words don't just go
    through the ears.

They can land on the heart
    and stay there for years.

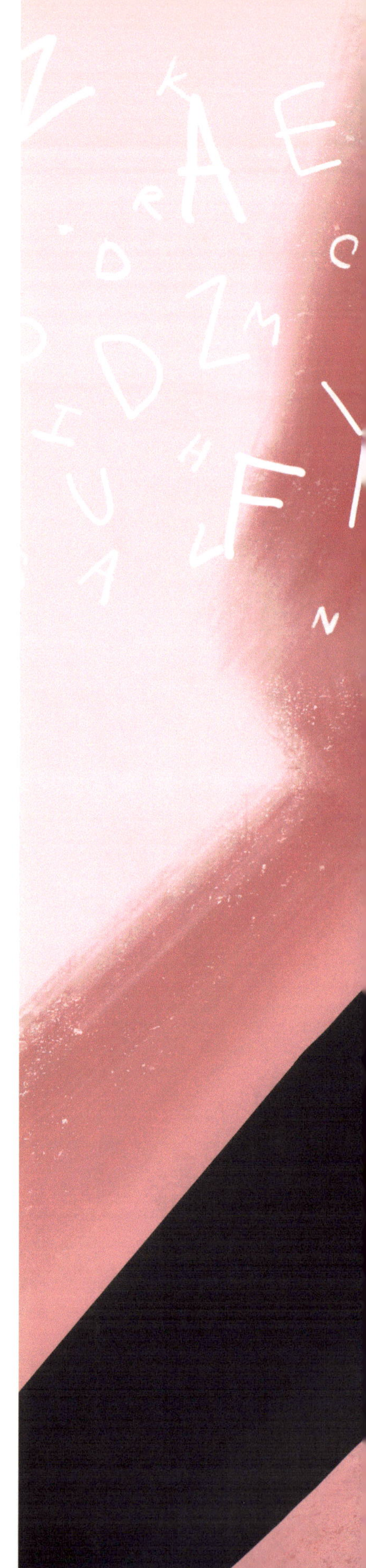

33

caring
kind
charming
honest
silly
gentle
curious
funny
confident
unique
adventurous
sweet
fair
loyal

There is another way to
check the words we say.

Imagine if the words you
said to Bentley came
back to you.

Same volume, same tone,
and same gestures, too.

Are they caring? Are they
kind? Are they true?

Okay, Grandma Grace,
    I think I need to practice.

Will you pretend to be Bentley and you
    bothered my game?

It is on a different level. Even my
    character's name was changed.

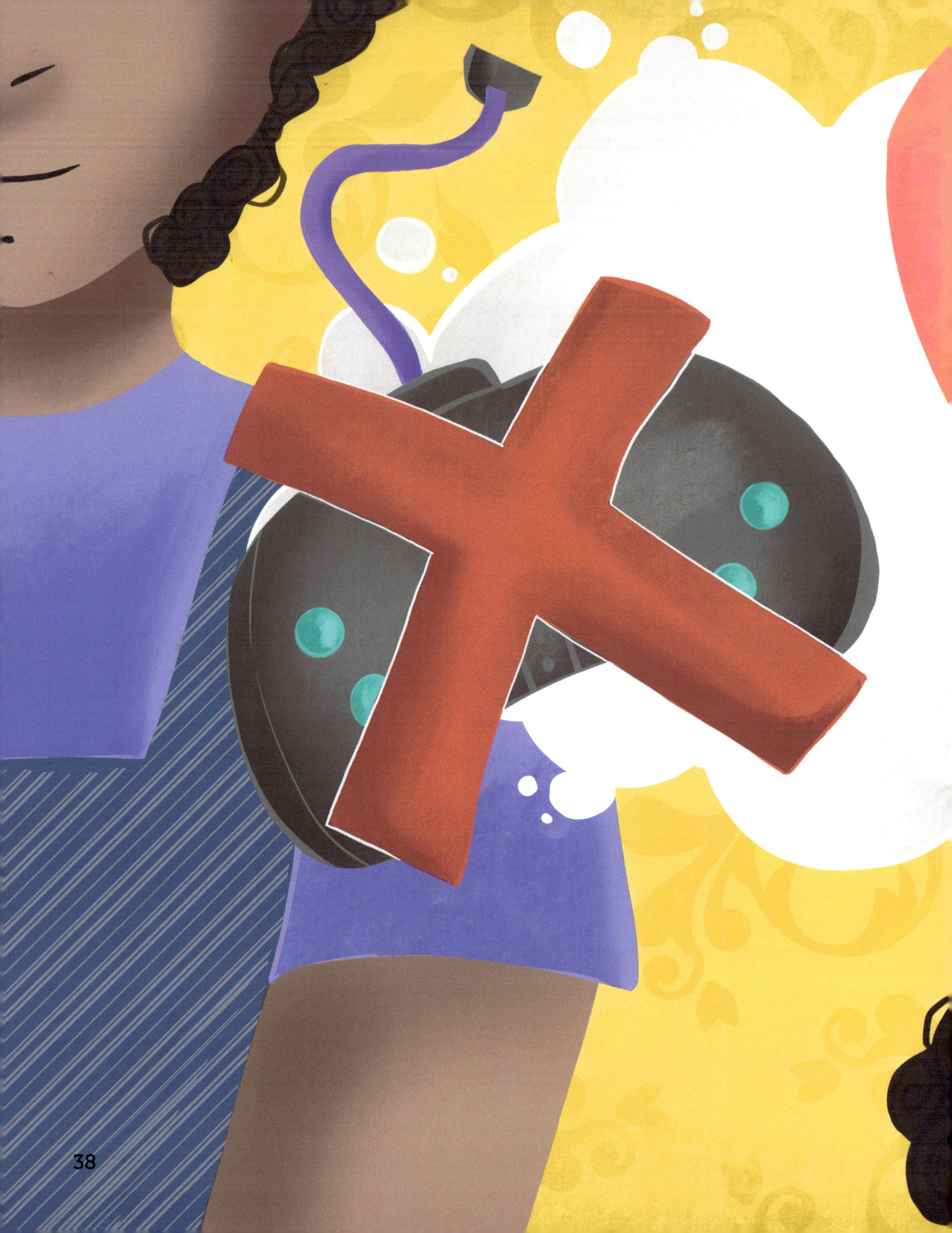

Of course! We'll go slow.

But there is something else
you should know.

When someone loves you,
your words mean more.

The words you say to Bentley
are more important than
your video game score.

Okay! Okay! I will say,
    Bentley, I don't like it
    when you bother my stuff.

But I am sorry that I said words
    that were mean and rough.

Let's both agree
    if you want to play,
just say, "Will you
spend some time
with me today?"

I will remember that the
words I say to Bentley
can stay with him
for years.

I will try not to say words
that will bring him
to tears.

I am so proud of you!
   And who knows?

If you two can learn to
   communicate, Bentley
   might become a fun little
   brother and a new playmate.

Practice a little every day.
   Before you speak, ask "is this
   really what I need to say."

Will you practice?

Yes! I can practice at school
and on the playground, too.

I'll try "Sample Your Words" with
my new friend, Sue.

lovely
serene

Then I will spread the word
to all my friends.

Maybe "Sample Your Words"
could start a kindness trend.

Sample Your Words
    and See How they Taste!

Do they tickle your tongue or do
    they burn your face?

Will they linger sweet like
    chocolate cake or will they grip
    and hurt like an old toothache?

Are they refreshing like a lemonade
    shower or are they strong and
    bitter like old cauliflower?

Words can bruise and words can
    burn or words can heal and
    show concern.

Sample Your Words
    and See How they Taste!

SOAP
53

Valeria V. Cordy Cray is a writer and retired educator. As a writer, her focus is on sharing memories, tenets, precepts, and prayers in the form of poetry, essays, and picture books. Her debut poetry book was **Following A Feather Trail**. This collection included the poem "Mother of My Mothers" which was awarded the Seaborn Jones Poetry Award. Val's grandmother's teaching had a profound influence in her life. One such teaching was to consider the power of your words. She currently lives in Lizella, Georgia with her husband Don.

Sabbath Canady is as an aspiring illustrator and writer. She enjoys watching movies and reading graphic novels. As a child, she wrote her first book, **Antwell's Dreams**, and hopes to continue writing in the future.

Sojourner Canady loves books and art. She is passionate about expressing herself, whether it be through art or other activities, and hopes to share that passion through her works.